THEN AND NOW ON THE GREAT NORTH

Volume 1

Deeside, Buchan, Speyside and the Shorter Branch Lines.

GRAHAM MAXTONE AND MIKE COOPER

© Graham Maxtone and Mike Cooper 2018
ISBN: 978-0902343-30-6

Published by the Great North of Scotland Railway Association, www.gnsra.org.uk
Printed in the United Kingdom by Henry Ling Limited, at the Dorset Press, Dorchester, DT1 1HD

Photograph Credits

The present day photographs were all taken by Dr Mike Cooper. Other photographers and sources are listed below, including those in the Association's Digital Archive Project.

Sir Malcolm Barclay-Harvey : 75 (Upper)

Colin Brown: 42, 75 (Lower)

John Diffey Collection : 76

Dr Bob Drummond : 8, 117, 119, 128, 119

Dr Ian Dunbar : 98, 121

Sandy Edward : 29

A G Ellis : 14, 88

Bill Emslie : front cover, 22, 53, 106

Dr John Emslie : 46, 81, 82, 139, 142, 146, 148 (Upper), 149, 152

A D Farr : 31 (Upper)

Keith Fenwick : 50 (Upper), 67

Hugo Fletcher : 31 (Lower)

R M Florence : 157, rear cover

Norris Forrest : 15, 38, 49, 62, 93, 101, 102, 105, 108, 126, 130, 133, 138, 144, 156

Alec Forsyth : 21

Jack Fraser via Rae Montgomery : 23

Sheila Gall : 19

John Spencer Gilks : 100

GNSRA Collection : 11, 16 (Lower), 20, 26, 27, 40, 41, 73 (Upper), 77, 85, 86, 96, 104, 110, 113, 114, 120, 134

Hugh Gordon : 36

Frank Guthrie : 57

Robin Hogg : 25

Douglas Hume : 28, 34, 83, 94, 123

R P Jackson : 91

Marion Johnstone, per Forbes and Catriona Young : 13

Ross Kerby/GNSRA Collection : 12, 17, 37, 65

C Lawson Kerr via Hamish Stevenson : 9

LGRP : 116, 159

J R Langford : 118

Graham E Langmuir : 132

Lens of Sutton Association : 33, 107, 115

Graham Maxtone Collection : 122, 137, 145, 151, 153, 155

L McKay : 18

Dr Mike Mitchell : 24

M A Mitchell - Jessie McHardy : 103

Mr and Mrs Moir : 6 (Lower)

Rae Montgomery : 125

Sandy Murdoch : 55, 58, 60, 61

Real Photographs : 158

Rev Dr George Booth Robertson : 30

Irvine Roy : 39

Jim Rule : 35 (Both)

Ian Sandison : 16 (Upper), 69, 112 (Lower)

W A C Smith (Transport Treasury) : 70, 71

Mike Stephen : 32, 44, 47, 48, 56, 64, 80, 84, 87, 124, 140, 141

James L Stevenson/Hamish Stevenson : 4, 10, 51, 54, 57 (Inset), 59, 63, 66, 68 (Lower), 72, 73 (Lower), 74, 78, 79, 89, 90, 92, 95, 97, 127, 129, 131 (insert), 150

G Norman Turnbull : 111, 112, 136, 143, 147, 148 (Lower), 154

Annie Watson : 50 (Lower)

Front Cover: A D40 hurries away from the terminus at **Banff** with a passenger train for the junction at Tillynaught where it will connect with the main line trains on the Moray Coast line. This evocative Bill Emslie watercolour depicts a crisp and clear winter scene from a hillside position above Scotstoun. The artist's keen attention to fine detail is apparent especially when compared with the same scene today. The cramped confines of the terminal can be fully appreciated from this angle which illustrates why the location can be a favourite amongst modellers who have limited space at their disposal. Although the permanent way and the station have vanished the track bed on the approach can easily be seen. It is also quite pleasing to note that many of the cottages have remained little changed.

CONTENTS

SOURCES AND BIBLIOGRAPHY

Great North Review, various issues

Great North of Scotland Railway - A Guide, W Ferguson of Kinmundy, David Douglas *(1881)*

Great North of Scotland Railway (2nd Edition), H A Vallance, House of Lochar *(1989)*

History of the Great North of Scotland Railway, Sir C M Barclay-Harvey, Ian Allan

The Great North of Scotland Railway, a New History, David Ross, Stenlake, 2015

Regional History of the Railways of Great Britain, Vol.15, J Thomas & D Turnock, House of Lochar

Great North Memories volumes 1, 2 (GNSR), 3 (LNER) and 4 (BR), GNSRA (1978, 1981, 1993 and 2014 respectively)

Little and Good, The Great North of Scotland Railway, Stephenson Locomotive Society (1972)

Great North of Scotland Railway Working Timetables 1911, GNSRA

The Royal Deeside Line, A D Farr, David & Charles (1968)

Stories of Royal Deeside's Railway, A D Farr, Kestrel Books (1971)

Royal Deeside's Railway, Dick Jackson, GNSRA (1999)

A Walk Along The Tracks, Hunter Davies, Weidenfeld & Nicolson (1982)

Railways of Buchan, Keith Fenwick, Douglas Flett and Dick Jackson , GNSRA (2008)

Peterhead Train, A G Murdoch, published by author

Walking The Line, Janet M McLeman, GNSRA (2015)

Rails to Alford, Dick Jackson, GNSRA (2006)

Rails to Banff, Macduff and Oldmeldrum, Duncan McLeish, GNSRA (2014)

The Speyside Line, A History and Guide, Dick Jackson and Keith Fenwick, GNSRA (2012)

Speyside Railways, Rosemary Burgess and Robert Kinghorn, Aberdeen University Press (1988)

Iron Rails and Whisky Trails, Ian Philip Peaty, Irwell Press (2013)

The Register of Scottish Signal Boxes, Forbes Alexander and Ed Nicoll, Herald Press (1988)

GNSRA Abstracts : 13 (Gradients,) 16 (Stations), 21 (Signalling), 31 (Bridges)

The Battery Railcar at **Aberdeen Joint** station in May 1964. Converted to battery operation from a Derby Lightweight unit at Cowlairs during 1957 the unit entered service on the Ballater branch on 28th March 1958. Three trips each way per day were timetabled for it and charging plants were provided at both Aberdeen and Ballater. In the early days it was equipped with side destination boards. It had mixed fortunes; it was very reliant on proper charging between trips and sensitive handling out on the line. It subsequently spent more time out of use than in operational service, especially after it was stabled overnight at Aberdeen instead of Ballater and it ceased to be used about 1962. Following official withdrawal sometime in 1966 it spent several years at Derby Research Centre repainted in red and blue livery and named *Gemini*. Thereafter in had various owners including the West Yorkshire Transport Museum and the East Lancashire Railway before moving to the Royal Deeside Railway Preservation Society at Crathes on 12th May 2006 where it now resides. As can be seen in the recent view, it has been restored to its original livery and the interior has been refurbished, albeit the centre front headlamp requires replacing. Currently it is hauled by the RDRPS's own motive power as battery operation has not yet been reinstated. Perhaps Elon Musk and Tesla with their successful electric cars have the solution waiting in the wings?

Introduction

Welcome to Volume 1 of *Then and Now on The Great North* which covers Deeside, Buchan, Speyside and the shorter branch lines. This publication became an aim of the Committee of the Great North of Scotland Railway Association when, as time went by, it became very apparent that the UK Past and Present series had come to an end without visiting our particular corner of north east Scotland.

The former Great North system suffered considerably both before and because of Dr Beeching, so much so that only 52 miles now remain of what was once an extensive rail network of about 335 miles. At its peak there were in excess of 160 stations in the north east and it is a very sobering thought that only six now remain for passengers. The reopening of Kintore will bring that up to seven.

As the world around us seems to be changing far more rapidly these days, there has been renewed interest in publications that compare the old with the new, be it railway, town or villages scenes. The Great North of Scotland Railway Association has an extensive archive of old photographs and slides so we had an abundance of material to work with. Consequently you might be excused for thinking that matching the old with the new would be pretty straightforward. However actually achieving this by getting in the exact spot a photographer stood some 50 or 60 years before can be a much bigger challenge than you might think. Trees or new buildings in the way, vantage points demolished and locations so drastically changed that distant landmarks had to be used to line up a suitably matching picture. In two cases the actual station buildings had been burned down after the photographic survey had been undertaken requiring an urgent re-visit!

One key element was of course finding the exact spots where the original photographs were taken and we would like to record our sincere gratitude and thanks to the many home and business owners who gave us full access to their properties so that the elusive perfect photograph could be taken. Many were extremely interested in and in some cases quite surprised at what their premises looked like all those years ago. We hope you enjoy this book and that it rekindles many happy memories from yesteryear.

Acknowledgments

The authors would like to sincerely thank Keith Fenwick for producing the introductions for each chapter and for his expert editing of the book, Keith Jones for proof reading and modifying the text accordingly and to them both for their wise and experienced counsel throughout.

The Lord Lieutenant of Aberdeenshire and the Chancellor, Rector and Principal of the University of Aberdeen prepare to meet royalty at **Holburn Street** on 27th September 1906. There is even a chap guarding the drinking fountain; woe betide

anyone who is thirsty. The Royal Train was due to arrive at 12.15 from Ballater but tradesmen are still putting finishing touches to the red carpet – cutting it a bit fine to say the least! The platform is all that survives of this scene today, and trees sprout where the dignitaries and tradesmen once stood and worked with haste. Graffiti now adorn the copes.

The westbound platform waiting room at **Holburn Street** with, in the centre, Mr Alexander Morrison, stationmaster from 1920 until 1928; he had already served in this capacity at Drum and Rathen. The highlight of his career at Holburn Street was on September 29th 1925, when King George V and Queen Mary alighted here

on their way to open an extension to Aberdeen Art Gallery. The shelter was larger than the standard style usually found on Great North stations no doubt befitting its status as a one time busy commuter station. Passengers for the west end would alight here and take a tram

into the city centre rather than go all the way to the Joint Station. This was the first stop out from Aberdeen and was closed with the withdrawal of the suburban trains in April 1937. There seems to be a distinct lack of trees where the waiting room was once located so perhaps some casual light digging might expose its former concrete base.

DEESIDE LINE

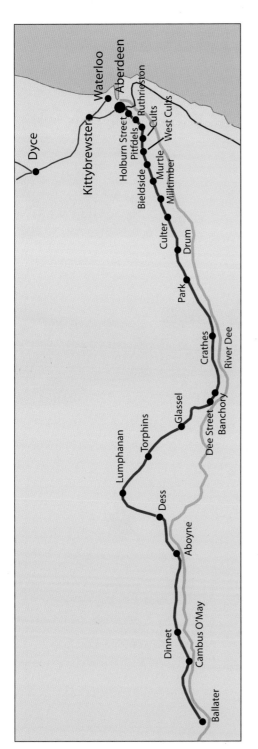

The Deeside Railway was for its first thirteen years completely independent of the Great North and in fact the section from Aberdeen to Banchory opened in 1853, the year before the line north from Aberdeen. Successive extensions to Aboyne in 1859 and Ballater in 1866 weakened it financially so it became part of the Great North system. A planned extension to Braemar would have run too close to Balmoral Castle so it was never built. Braemar was served from 1904 by the Great North's first motor bus service. At the other end of the line, a frequent suburban service operated as far as Culter from 1887.

For many years, the line was busy, especially as far as Banchory. It carried residential traffic from as far away as Ballater and hordes of Aberdonians on day trips in summer. The Culter service ceased in 1937 and use of the other services declined. Revival came in the form of diesel railcars and the unique battery railcar in the late 1950s. However this was not enough to save the line from the Beeching cuts and it closed in 1966.

The Deeside Way for walkers and cyclists runs from Aberdeen to Ballater partly on the course of the line – see deesideway.org. Much of the line from Aboyne to Ballater is walkway, with a particularly attractive stretch by the Dee at Cambus O'May. From Crathes there is a path to the outskirts of Banchory beside the Royal Deeside Railway Preservation Society's line. This provides an opportunity to ride part of the Deeside line – see deeside-railway.co.uk for more details.

The Royal Carriage at Holburn Station, 27/9/06

The view from Gray Street on 27th September 1906 was taken not long after the photograph on page 6 and shows the King and Queen leaving **Holburn Street** station *en route* to open the new buildings at Marischal College. As befits the occasion

the streets are thronging with local people keen to see their Monarch and the obligatory Guard of Honour stands to attention. The station is in the top right hand side of the photograph and if you look carefully you can just make out the carriage roofs of the Royal Train and the roof of the down platform waiting shelter. The street level building on the left is still there albeit modified and the granite retaining wall leading to the east bridge abutment looks as good as the day it was built. The railway bridge has been replaced by a new and very different version for walkers and cyclists only. Illustrated on the right is the cover of the programme for the visit. Other pages gave details of the procession.

CITY OF ABERDEEN.

VISIT OF

Their Majesties the King and Queen

TO ABERDEEN,

ON THE OCCASION OF THE

Opening of the New Buildings at Marischal College,

27th SEPTEMBER, 1906.

OFFICIAL PROGRAMME.

Class B12 No.61543 accelerates through the former suburban station at **Ruthrieston** with the 10.10am Aberdeen to Ballater train in July 1952. By that date, trains stopped at all stations on the route. The platforms are still in existence. As with Holburn Street and the other suburban stations Ruthrieston closed in April 1937. Such was the decline in people using the 'subbies' it had become a Halt in June 1927. Today the Deeside way occupies the former track bed. The boundary fence and public road are still there although the fence has been renewed recently.

The former suburban station at **Pitfodels** seen on 5th May 1954; the down line on the left was closed in 1951. The station building is a standard Great North wooden structure that could be found throughout the system and it still survives today as a dwelling house in very good order. Despite a modern extension and internal rebuild, many of the original external design features have been kept and due credit must be given to the architect. It is quite coincidental that there is a dog in almost exactly the same spot in each photo, albeit a different breed.

The stationmaster Mr Walker, his staff and intending passengers pose for the camera in this view of **Cults** looking towards Aberdeen in the 1920s. Cults was fortunate in surviving the cull of suburban stations in 1937 and remained until the Deeside line closed to passengers in February 1966. Happily the main station building is extant and has been used as a joiner's workshop for many years. It should be noted that the former open waiting area had been enclosed during its railway operational life sometime after the original photograph was taken. The extension at the west end of the building was built after closure. The location of the former platform clock can still be easily identified.

CULTS HOTEL AND POST OFFICE   GREAT NORTH OF SCOTLAND RAILWAY   Porter, Photo., Aberdeen

A Great North of Scotland Railway postcard of the Hotel and Post Office at **Cults**. This clearly shows how the structure and associated buildings have remained basically unchanged and only added to and extended to meet increasing demands. The old buildings on the left have been replaced by flats and the main road has been realigned.

An old glass plate gives us this excellent picture of a down suburban passenger train sitting at **West Cults** sometime before 1919. In fairly sharp detail are the lower quadrant semaphore signal on its wooden post, the Great North footbridge and eight wire telephone pole. The westbound platform station building is just visible to the left of the coaches. No signal box/block post was provided here, only a ground frame on the platform operated by the stationmaster who had instructions to place signals to danger after a train arrived in the platform and only clear them again once it had departed. These signals were removed in April 1919. Note the short treads at the side of the signal post to allow an agile signal lineman to gain access to the arm and lenses for maintenance; the actual lamp would have been worked by a windlass. Today the

underbridge at the end of the old station has been replaced by a fairly substantial footbridge and the footpath meanders west along the trackbed between the site of the former platforms. The recent view was taken nearer the old station due to access constraints.

A westbound suburban train pulls away from its booked stop at **Bieldside**. At least seven Great North coaches are visible. Although the suburban trains ceased as long ago as 1937 you do wonder, in these more enlightened times, how successful such a service would be for today's commuters into the city. The only identifiable feature in the recent view is Bieldside Road overbridge in the middle distance. Although the stonework is original the metalwork decking has been renewed.

The suburban station of **Murtle** in September 1969, by which time the main building was in private ownership, extended at the back and with a caravan alongside. Although it has some recognisable Great North features it was not a standard building, especially the short canopy on the platform side, as the original building had been destroyed by fire on 17th August 1909. In today's view the main building has been further extended and the canopy, along with its supporting decorative metalwork, still survives as does the former platform made with solid Aberdeenshire granite. The agent's house is visible on the left.

A family on holiday pose for the camera, albeit a bit self consciously, in front of the LNER Camping Coach in the sidings at **Murtle**. We can speculate as to who they all are but it could possibly be mother, father, mother-in-law, father-in-law and daughter with the daughter's husband taking the photo for posterity.

The gentlemen are all in shirts and ties which was fairly typical of the holiday uniform in those far off happy days. Standard deck chairs complete the scene. How many families enjoyed holidays at this excellent location? Only the memories remain in today's overgrown scene (right). Camping Coaches were widespread throughout the Great North and indeed the United Kingdom from the 1930s to 1960s.

A busy scene at **Milltimber** (below) looking east in GNS days. A six coach eastbound service has just departed and a westbound one is arriving. There is another standard Great North station building with the Stationmaster's house just visible behind. Note the ladder lying against the lamp bracket ready for the late shift porter to fire up the platform light. Judging by the ash ballast thrown up onto the eastbound platform ramp it looks like the foot crossing in the foreground is getting some refurbishment. Today (above) vegetation encroaches almost the entire area except for the footpath/cycle way in the former track bed.

Railway Station, Culter

A tinted postcard of **Culter** in Great North days looking east with a westbound passenger train arriving. The signal box is just in view on the left and the original Great North wooden footbridge frames the view. Culter was generally as far as the suburban trains went with only a handful going on to Banchory. In the summer of 1914, the zenith of rail traffic on Deeside, between suburban, through passenger trains and goods traffic Culter saw 36 westbound and 35 eastbound trains in every 17 hour working day – nearly 4 trains per hour. There was a short branch to Culter Paper Mills which trailed off the eastbound line just to the left of the picture and it survived along with the station until 2nd January 1967. Today the eastbound platform is remarkably well preserved but Station Road bridge which crossed in the middle of the two platforms has gone, as has the westbound platform. The stone abutments for the bridge remain though.

A westbound seven coach passenger train for Ballater pulls away from **Culter** on the 1 in 80 gradient towards the 8½ milepost. The Culter Up Home signal is visible above the fourth carriage. It was very difficult to get exactly the same angle here today hence the fact that the houses behind the train are not seen in today's photograph, but they are still there. What ties the two scenes in perfectly are the retaining walls and bridges that still survive. This view was at its best after the leaves had fallen in Autumn.

The two platform station at **Drum** looking east about 1926 with the signal box at the end of the eastbound platform. Following the closure of the suburban stations by the LNER in 1937 Drum was the next casualty being closed for both passenger and goods by British Railways in September 1951. The main building was again of a standard Great North wooden design as was the small waiting room, mostly hidden by the footbridge, on the westbound platform. The platforms are partly visible today but, more importantly and remarkably, so too is the old westbound platform waiting room although it has been turned to face the other way by its new owner and serves as a summerhouse (inset).

The GNSR built a bridge over the River Dee to facilitate access to **Park** station for those living on the south side of the river. Of course, they charged for this facility and this photo, dated 1897, shows the toll keepers cottage and we believe, his two wee girls. Perhaps their relatives would one day be able to let us know the names of these two wee tooties!

Track lifting at **Park** in October 1970 with the contractors shunting engine hauling wagonloads of track panels which await unloading by the roadside crane. The station building looks understandably unkempt as it is now nearly five years since closure; the poster advertising the withdrawal of passenger services barely clings to the wall beside the ticket office window and the weeds are beginning to take over the permanent way. Today the building is the office for Dee Valley Caravans. Although recognisable it has been renovated and extended quite considerably but the chimney pots are still the same. Caravans sit where the shunting engine stood over 45 years before.

A Bill Emslie watercolour of an eastbound goods powering through **Crathes** in the winter twilight during British Railways days. In today's view all is not what it seems. The signal box here was closed in 1954 and the wooden top wooden half removed. However following closure of the line the station was owned for some years by the internationally acclaimed silversmith and engraver Malcolm Appleby. He rebuilt the upper section of the signal box to the original plans and there it sits today.

A general view of the station and yard at **Crathes** looking east in 1949. A Camping Coach was based here at one time. The yard looks quite busy with wagons in every siding so it is hoped that shunting operations did not disturb the holidaymakers. Crathes closed to goods in June 1964 and completely along with the passenger services in February 1966. Today the passenger platforms are just visible in the undergrowth but little evidence remains of the former goods yard. The Royal Deeside Railway Preservation Society has its own short section of track and new station a little further west of here, as illustrated on page 98.

A general view of **Banchory** from the road above the station which was taken after closure and before vandalism took over. The weeds are starting to grow along the sides of the building and general decay is beginning to set in. What looks like snow in the hollow at the bottom right hand side of the photo is actually a by-product from the generation of acetylene gas for the station within the wooden building alongside. How was the by-product finally disposed of? The transformation today is immediately apparent.

This colour shot was taken from the eastbound platform at **Banchory** and shows the well appointed waiting rooms and offices on the westbound platform. Note the supporting columns with elaborate decoration and the acetylene gas lamps suspended from the roof of the canopy. After the final trains ran Banchory suffered from the almost inevitable vandalism that affected nearly every closed station and the platforms became a sea of broken glass. A heart-breaking end for those that knew the station so well in its heyday. Today the entire area has been built over and no trace remains except for the road bridge behind the cameraman which gave access to the goods yard at the west end of the old platforms.

Mr Clark the stationmaster, the contractor and his foreman pose for the camera in front of the new station at **Banchory** during its rebuilding in 1902. Note the contractor's traction engine behind. When the work was finished Banchory had a substantial station with a commodious main building, canopies on both platforms, an enclosed footbridge and a large waiting room on the westbound platform. Today this once proud station has been wiped off the face of the map. The only point of reference is the West Manse on the hill above the houses built on the station site.

The wooden halt at **Dee Street** opened on 6th February 1961 to encourage passenger usage. It was closer to the centre of Banchory and accessed by a steep flight of stairs from the road. A single oil lamp on the platform for illumination after dark and two running in boards were the only enhancements to this basic halt; not even a seat was provided. This was the shortest lived station on Deeside, lasting just over five years. Today no trace of the halt and its access staircase remains.

A colour view of **Glassel** looking east which was taken by Douglas Hume on 9th October 1965 in the months leading up to passenger closure. The station had become unstaffed by this time but looked in reasonable condition, no doubt due to its rural location. Note that the Great North running in board has had a British Railways blue enamel replacement fixed over the top of it – a common feature at many north east stations. The small yard with its loading bank on the right had already been lifted following closure to goods just over a year previously. The hut which contained the ground frame for operating the yard points is still *in situ* at the east end of the platform. The closure notice is on display in the west facing window at the gable end. The station building remains today and like almost every Deeside station of this recognisable design has been converted and considerably extended into a substantial private house with well kept grounds.

The general outline of the old building is recognisable and, looking closely, the old chimney pots are still there!

A Sandy Edwards shot of **Torphins** looking towards Ballater taken from the rear of a departing Battery Railcar working to Aberdeen on 11th April 1960. Alighting passengers are leaving the station and the signalman with tablet pouch over his shoulder ambles back to the signal box to replace the signals and set up the road for the next train. Like most Deeside stations, Torphins was very well kept. It had the apparent luxury of a second footbridge, just out of sight behind the camera, which was a right of way for the good folk of the village before the railway came. Looking at today's view you can probably see why it was very difficult to establish the same location as no trace of the station remains, although the road bridge in the distance still survives.

The five-arch **Balnacraig Viaduct,** often referred to as **Beltie Viaduct** as it crossed the burn of that name, was on the stiff 1 in 70 climb to the cutting at Satan's Den. A steam hauled service is crossing over *en route* to Ballater. This was taken by the Rev George Booth Robertson and donated to the Great North Association by his son; it is one of only three known photographs of steam crossing the viaduct. Following closure of the line and despite a vigorous campaign to save it, including support by local Grampian TV personality John Duncanson, Beltie Viaduct was very sadly demolished in 1989. From the same standpoint today even the void left by this incredibly crass action cannot be seen although the minor road and the stub of the embankment on the left are still there.

Looking west through the quarter of a mile long and 50ft deep cutting at Tillychin between Torphins and Lumphanan known as **'Satan's Den'**. 97,000 cubic yards of earth were excavated here during construction of the line. The photograph on the right was taken from the cab of a DMU and the one below after closure but before track lifting as it shows the weeds are beginning to set in. You can imagine a fierce north east blizzard howling across and filling in the cutting here with drifting snow very easily. At 611ft feet above sea level, it must have been a miserable place on the footplate of a steam engine during extreme winter conditions. No wonder it was called Satan's Den. In today's view, below right, trees have taken over, the bridge has been removed and the cutting filled in.

The station and passing loop at the neat station of **Lumphanan** looking towards Ballater on 26th February 1966. The station buildings look remarkably fresh in green and cream and the footbridge in green and grey shows a variation to the standard black or sometimes grey paint used for these structures. Note what looks like a very short siding coming off the eastbound loop on the right. This was provided to catch any breakaways from eastbound loose-coupled goods trains struggling up the climb to Satan's Den cutting. Once an eastbound goods had departed the Lumphanan signalman would turn these points to the run off position as a precaution to ensure any runaways did not roll back into the section towards Aboyne. Today you might be forgiven for thinking that the former station building had been converted into a bungalow. Unfortunately not in this instance, it only shares the general outline of the former structure. The distant chimney pots help lock the two views.

The somewhat isolated station of **Dess** taken from a westbound service train in LNER days. The porter has collected the limited mail from the guard and seems to be hurrying up three intending passengers to get on board. Note the old platform oil lamp with the station names fixed to the glass; the one nearest the camera has seen better days. The station building is another of the standard design for Deeside stations. Most of it was a dwelling house; only two rooms formed the actual office and waiting room. The building is still there in private ownership albeit partially hidden by bushes and the wooden lamp post has been replaced by a cast iron version of a different style. The platform can still be seen and a healthy pile of firewood occupies the spot where the running in board and seat were.

The impressive station at **Aboyne** looking east in the early 1960s. The signals have been raised for a train to Aberdeen and the signalman is walking along the platform to meet its arrival and change the tablets. The porter is chatting to the one intending passenger and he has some mail bags at his feet ready to load. Well-tended small flower beds complement the scene. The station was rebuilt in the late 1890s and only the stone-built goods shed survived from the original layout. Today the main station building is owned by Aberdeenshire Council and let out for private use, including an excellent café. The basic fabric of the building has been very well restored even down to replicating the style of the original windows and doors. The canopies, footbridge, platforms, track and signals have vanished without a trace.

(Above) In a careful blend of then and now at **Aboyne** a cheery group comprising from left to right Messrs P and I Wright and the station porter A Littlejohn pose in front of the bookstall run by Mrs Tawse. The nearest man is wearing an ex-army blouson jacket. These items of clothing were a common sight in those days and lasted their owners many years upon their return to normal working life. The bookstall itself is well stocked and was very likely the news outlet for the village as well as intending passengers. Platform fixtures and fittings include a chocolate machine, the standard benches and a sign proclaiming 'General and Ladies 3rd Class Waiting Rooms'.

(Above) The **Aboyne** signalman poses in front of J36 0-6-0 No.65251 and his cabin during a pause in shunting operations. This engine was built in 1892 and survived until withdrawal at Bathgate in July 1964, an impressive 72 years of service. The shirt sleeves and the open window indicate that summer is here. To identify and capture the same location today was very difficult but here it is on the left. The signalman and his box have gone as has 65251 and its driver.

Passenger trains cross at **Dinnet** on 4th August 1932. The late Hugh Gordon fortunately recorded details of the trains – the express from Aberdeen on the right and the slow from Ballater on the left crossing at 5.49pm. The level crossing gates are closed to road traffic and will have been shut for a while as the eastbound train has already arrived and the signal has been cleared ready for the Ballater service to depart. Having said that there doesn't appear to be any vehicles waiting patiently. Dinnet had a very small yard with a loading bay and head shunt; timber was often despatched from here. The road is of course still there today as is the station building, which is used as estate offices, but the tree growth through the platforms makes it nigh on impossible to get any other form of comparable view. However the concrete base of the goods shed on the extreme left is still there.

An up passenger service with at least nine coaches begins to brake for its station stop at **Dinnet** in Great North days. The train has just passed the distant signal which is in the clear position (note the wire in the foreground) so it will be right away for Aberdeen as soon as station duties are completed. The track bed forms a very pleasant footpath today and the old boundary fences are still intact although not so well maintained. The trees in the original shot will surely have been felled and the forest re-planted again. Although the railway has gone the cycle of life continues.

Cambus O'May looking west in the 1950s, a tidy single platform station with a neat little office cum waiting room. It was and still is a delightful location situated beside the River Dee. It must have been a real pleasure to wait for the train here on a nice summer's afternoon. The former yard connection veered away to the right where pink granite from the quarry at Tomnakiesk was loaded at one time. Gunpowder for the quarry was also shipped in by rail. The loading bank to the right of the old Great North coach body used to have a short siding which at one time held a camping coach, but this was transferred to Aboyne sometime after nationalisation of the railways in 1947. A group of Deeside Way hikers pose for the camera in roughly the same spot as the visiting enthusiasts in the old photograph. The platform, tastefully renovated station

building, now a holiday home, and granite built loading bank are still very much in existence today. The body of the old coach has long gone and all that remains are a few bits of its base slowly rotting away.

A group in contemporary clothing wait for the train at **Cambus O'May** in 1928. The gentleman in uniform and wearing the flat cap is the then stationmaster Alexander Roy. He had started there in 1924 so will have been in charge for 4 years by the time the photograph was taken. In an interesting departure from the normal 'then and now' composition in today's view we have, standing in the same spot, Alexander Roy's grandson Irvine, a retired railwayman of long and distinguished service. Not only that but Mr Roy is wearing the very same flat cap his grandfather was wearing in the original 1928 shot. Mr Roy's grandmother Maggie was placed in charge at Cambus O'May after her husband's death and worked there until it became unstaffed in 1956. Quite remarkable.

A two-car Metro-Cammell Diesel Multiple Unit pulls away from its stop at **Cambus O'May** with the 6.08pm from Aberdeen *en route* to its final destination at Ballater on 18th June 1960. The Gordon Suspension Bridge over the Dee is on the right and access to it from the road is over the railway just at the end of the station platform. Today the railway retaining wall on the riverside and the bridge are easily identifiable, although the approach span on the north side was changed to allow direct access from the Deeside Way when the bridge was refurbished in 1985. The bridge was badly damaged in the severe flood of the river in December 2015 and still awaits repair and re-opening at the time of publication.

Station Square at **Ballater** in the 1930s with a wide selection of vehicles, including an Alexander's bus, parked randomly. The substantial wooden station building is on the left and just visible in the distance is the roof of the four-road Royal Train carriage shed. The granite Victoria and Albert Halls complete the scene on the right. Looking at the same view on 26th May 2014 you might be forgiven for thinking that the railway still served Ballater. However the station building housed the Tourist Information Office and Visitor Centre complete with replica Victorian Royal Railway carriage, council offices, restaurant and shops. A confectioners shop and trees block the view to the site of the now demolished carriage sheds.

A close up view of the west end of the station building with dining and tearoom at **Ballater** in 1955 showing the ornate design of the building and its hexagonal roofline. Note too the large railway sign fixed to the roof which loudly proclaims 'British Railways Ballater'. In the lower view on 26th October 2014, the lack of any real change can clearly be noted. Although the former British Railways sign on the roof has been removed its supporting framework is still there and the shop and restaurant look welcoming in their red and cream paintwork.

As a postscript to the previous photographs the old station at **Ballater** was severely damaged by fire on 12th May 2015. Although the building was almost completely destroyed, the replica Royal Carriage was saved relatively unscathed thanks to the valiant efforts of the fire fighters. The upper photograph taken on 26th May 2014 contrasts with the middle from 14th May 2015. Rebuilding in traditional style was due to be completed in Spring 2018; the work is almost complete in the lower view from Station Square taken in late April 2018. Compare this view with those on page 41.

The Buchan line platform at **Dyce** looking towards Aberdeen in 1964. Dyce boasted four platform faces at this time and was the only junction station on the Great North system that had two platforms for its branch. A substantial footbridge spanned all four tracks. The imposing Type 1 signal box stands in the gap between the Main and Buchan lines. From the same standpoint today the Buchan platforms and associated tracks have gone and the gap has been filled in to form parking for the local commuters. All the former station buildings and the footbridge have been removed. The main building on the left lasted longest as it was converted into a chip shop but it burnt down and has subsequently been replaced. A new footbridge, which incorporates lifts for ease of access, connects the surviving main line platforms. New modern waiting shelters have also been provided which are bright and far too airy. The signal box is still there for now and retains many of its original features following renovation a few years ago.

BUCHAN LINES

The Buchan lines were an important source of traffic for the Great North, serving a rich agricultural area and the important fishing ports of Fraserburgh and Peterhead. Starting from Dyce on the main line, a fairly direct route was followed to Fraserburgh. Peterhead was served by a branch from Maud to avoid the higher ground in central Buchan. After these lines were completed in the 1860s, Maud became a major centre for the cattle trade with a large auction mart which required the operation of many special livestock trains. The importance of Fraserburgh and Peterhead grew, particularly after the introduction of steam trawlers. Special trains delivered fish to London overnight and the line was particularly busy during the herring season.

Two branches were constructed. The Cruden line from Ellon was built in the 1890s, in part to serve the large hotel built by the GNSR at Cruden Bay. It terminated at Boddam, not far from Peterhead. Repeated calls for it to be extended there went unheeded so the line closed to passengers in 1932 and to goods in 1945.

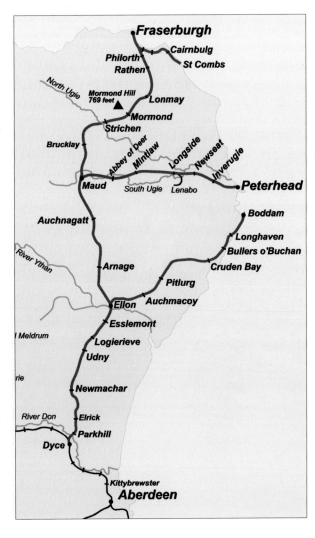

From Fraserburgh, a light railway was opened in 1903 along the coast to St. Combs. It was always busy with local traffic and still had a frequent service on closure in 1965.

Passenger traffic, particularly to Peterhead, suffered badly from bus competition so it was little surprise that the whole line from Dyce was proposed for closure in the Beeching Plan. Passenger trains ceased in 1965, with goods traffic continuing to Peterhead until 1970 and Fraserburgh until 1979. Since then, the trackbed has been converted into the popular Formartine & Buchan Way for use by walkers and cyclists.

Many buildings remain, converted to domestic use. At Maud a small railway museum has been established, currently open one weekend each month.

Parkhill, just over a mile from Dyce, was the first station on the Buchan line and was an early victim of closure, losing its passenger service in April 1950. The photograph above, looking north, was taken on 24th August 1957. The connection to the yard looks disused although goods traffic continued until August 1961. The remains of the passenger platform can still be seen. A signal box was opened in May 1920 when a short section of double line of just over a mile long was provided between here and Elrick. This was used during the summer months only until August 1925 when it was permanently closed and the double line again reduced to single track. Today the underbridge in the foreground has been replaced by a footbridge which forms part of the Formartine & Buchan Way.

Newmachar looking north towards Udny on 25th August 1957. Although the station is still operational the unkempt condition of the platforms and general surroundings suggest that only the signal box is now manned. A standard LNER footbridge which replaced the earlier GNSR all wood version frames the scene. The LNER versions were built using old bullhead rail, wood and signal wire and served the north east country stations well during their lifetime. Renovated examples remain at Insch and Huntly. Another, which was originally at Longmorn, is now at Aviemore but no longer in use. Today Newmachar's station building has been converted into a house and both platforms remain *in situ*.

A superb Mike Stephen colour shot of a southbound train hauled by a North British Locomotive Type 2 (later Class 21) and comprised of ex-LMS coaches calling at **Udny** in October 1965, just before the withdrawal of passenger services. The signalman is exchanging tokens with the driver and no doubt swapping the news of the day at the same time. Meanwhile the guard is at the back of the train keen to give the right away but probably tolerant of the time taken to exchange the almost obligatory gossip. But that was just part of the daily routine in the old days of the country railway. Today the platforms are still there, the one on the right now being part of the gardens of adjacent houses. The road bridge at the end still survives but the train, the people and the old traditions have sadly long gone.

The neat little single platform wayside station at **Logierieve** looking south, photographed by Norris Forrest in the 1960's. It was known as Newburgh Road when it opened in July 1861 but that only lasted for about 3 months! Although there is a signal box on the platform it had not been used as a block post since as long ago as 1894 and served only as a covered ground frame to operate the siding points. Goods facilities were withdrawn in November 1960. Unusually and more in keeping with the traditions of the Highland Railway only alternate platform copes are whitened. The station building still survives today and like many others has been converted into an extended dwelling house. The old clock face is still there.

Although it had been closed to all traffic since September 1952 the station, already converted into a house, and platform at **Esslemont** were still there when this north facing view was taken in July 1969. Even more surprising both the building and platform are still there in 2017. Esslemont did have a signal box and crossing loop but these were removed in September 1925. The Association had the pleasure of recording the memories of Annie Watson whose father was once a leading porter here. She produced a photograph of a derailment north of the station. It was subsequently established that this took place on 26th October 1910. North of Esslemont, the line rose at 1 in 248, followed by a short level section, then it fell at 1 in 75 towards Ellon. The 5.15am goods train from Kittybrewster to Maud split into two at the

summit. The rear portion then picked up speed in the same direction and collided with the front section of the train with some force. The derailment killed 18 of the 35 cattle on board. The two open wagons which were badly damaged contained merchandise for Maud and New Deer areas which can be seen piled on the embankment. It included barrels of apples, boxes of herring, and casks of treacle. Over 200 yards of track were damaged. The only brakes would have been on

the engine and the guard's van. An expensive accident for the cash-strapped GNSR.

Ellon looking north in the 1950s. Thompson B1 No.61242 *Alexander Reith Gray* shunts empty coaching stock in the yard behind the old Boddam line platform. The rather substantial building on the right was built with the Boddam branch in mind as ticket offices and waiting rooms, just in view on the left were also provided on the northbound platform. Today the platforms can still be seen but all buildings have been removed and the yard is a council depot with a new office block under construction when photographed. The proposal to reinstate the line from Dyce to Ellon is gathering support at the time of writing no doubt further encouraged by the success of the reopened Borders Railway.

Arnage looking towards Maud and Fraserburgh with the north signal box in the distance. The crossing loop and signal boxes were removed here some nine months before withdrawal of the passenger services and curiously it was the platform on the right, the former up loop, that was used until closure. After the line closed completely the surviving main building on the northbound platform was converted into a house and extended towards the old platform edge and at the sides. The Formartine & Buchan Way passes by on the old track bed.

A fine Bill Emslie watercolour showing **Auchnagatt** looking towards Maud in 1915. An attractive, compact country station with its main building, wooden footbridge, up platform waiting room and main signal box grouped together. The goods yard came off the northbound loop immediately after the signal that can be seen at the platform end. All the railway buildings and footbridge were removed after passenger closure and before the good trains finished in October 1979. Subsequently a bungalow has been built on the site of the northbound platform main building and a small boundary wall erected along the old platform edge. The southbound platform is also still there, almost hidden behind the very tall trees on the right.

The southern approach to **Maud** on 24th April 1965 showing the junction, yard connection and storage sidings in the distance on the right. This was where northbound passenger trains would stop and divide with one portion moving to the Fraserburgh platform and the other to that for Peterhead. Trees obliterate this scene completely today. The base of the water tower can still be found in the undergrowth.

A lengthy Peterhead bound goods train hauled by Type 2 diesel (later Class 24) D5070 changes tokens with the **Maud** signalman as it passes through the station *en route* to its destination. At that time at least two goods trains a day served Peterhead where the Cross & Blackwell factory was a considerable source of traffic. In contrast, at the same location, a fork-lift unloads a restored former Peterhead Prison wagon for static display at Maud Railway Museum on 1st September 2016. Details on the Museum and its opening days can be found at friendsofmaud. org.uk.

Emitting a puff of oily black smoke D6152, a North British Locomotive Company product later Class 21, moves away from its coaches which it has just placed in the Peterhead platform at **Maud** to run round ready for the trip back to Peterhead on 1st May 1965. This was one of the very last passenger trains to Peterhead. Although trains traditionally split and combined at Maud, by this time they ran to Fraserburgh with connecting shuttles to Peterhead. The yard in the background is unusually quiet but signs of fresh straw dropped from the loading bank indicate that potato traffic has been loaded recently. The same scene today shows all passenger platforms still intact as well as the main station buildings where Maud Railway Museum is now located. The Peterhead Prison wagon seen in the previous picture has now been positioned in the former Fraserburgh platform and within the small compound more sleepers, chairs and track await relaying by volunteers. The North British built Class 21 was the mainstay of loco hauled passenger services on the Buchan lines but it is well documented that they were not the

most reliable form of the new age diesel traction. They were built at their Springburn works in Glasgow and each was adorned with four of the companies instantly recognisable diamond shaped builders plates. An example from D6152 is shown inset.

The last railwayman at **Maud**, Jim Morrison, poses proudly carrying his badge of office, the shunting pole, in 1979. Mr Morrison was the last signalman at Maud when it was finally switched out on 5th March 1969 and therefore had the unenviable distinction of being the very last signalman in Buchan. He started as a Junior Porter at Auchterless on 23rd May 1932 and, like many north east railwaymen, moved around to get promotion to such places as Newmacher, Pitcaple and Fraserburgh before finishing at Maud after 43 years service on 8th December 1979. Jim is shown inset at Fraserburgh in front of the Tyer's Key Token machine. Note the old waiting area in the background, the ticket office window on the right and the clock face on the outside wall without hands, the general clutter and weeds on the platform, all the signs of a once proud and busy country junction in decline. Fast forward to 2018 and standing in front of the building is Jim Morrison's son Ian re-creating his Dad's 1979 pose. The building and old booking office have been renovated, as can be seen by the now well cared-for environs.

Type 2 D5357, later Class 27, with the 12.20 Aberdeen to Fraserburgh on 29th March 1965 awaits the right of way for Fraserburgh once station duties have been completed. This locomotive had come up to Aberdeen on a passenger service from Glasgow Buchanan Street earlier in the day and was working a fill in turn to Fraserburgh and back before returning south. Today's view shows the renovated prison van and a Royal Naval Dockyard wagon. The different levels of the Fraserburgh and Peterhead platforms are quite noticeable.

Brucklay looking north in September 1953. A very solid looking stone building occupies the northbound platform along with the standard GNSR Type 2b signal box. The flat-roofed brick built store was a later addition. The standard small waiting room, or verandah as they were usually referred to, is provided on the southbound platform. The station gardens are well kept and there are even floral display boxes on the ledges of the store windows. The station also served as the local Post Office at one time. Today the station has been converted like so many others on the line into a dwelling house but not only that, the former store has been renovated as well, possibly as a workshop cum tool shed. Just as at Auchnagatt boundary fence has been built along the old platform edge.

A southbound passenger train which includes several fish vans runs into **Brucklay** in LNER days behind a former North British Railway Class D31 4-4-0. As an economy measure the signalling arrangements were modified in July 1932 so that Brucklay signal box could be switched out of circuit and closed at quieter times. The adjacent signal boxes at Maud and Strichen would then work to each other with the signals at Brucklay cleared for trains in both directions. The yard connections come in from the left and it remained operational after the signal box shut in June 1959, worked by a ground frame. Looking north today the old fence can still be seen whilst the stone Aucheoch overbridge stands proudly at the start of the cutting. The area once occupied by the goods yard, which was shut on 28th March 1966, has been fenced off and is under private ownership.

Hauled by Class 25 No.25085 the last remnants of Buchan goods traffic rumbles on to the viaduct over the North Ugie Water just south of **Strichen** on 31st August 1977 with an Aberdeen bound working. A parcels van and Freightliner container can be seen in the consist but there will be precious little else. Happily this was one location where a relatively uninterrupted view of the former scene could be photographed and not only that, the bridge is still there. The paint has all flaked off now and trees and bushes are starting to sprout and grow out of the stonework but otherwise the structure has not changed other than the lifting of the rails.

Norris Forrest took this colour shot of the wayside station at **Strichen** looking north on 1st November 1964. A stiff climb to Mormond at a ruling gradient of 1 in 66 lay ahead for Fraserburgh-bound trains. As with the majority of Great North country stations all is neat and tidy. The crossing loop here could accommodate trains of no greater than 25 wagons (525ft). Closed to passengers on 4th October 1965 goods facilities were kept until 19th June 1967. The signal box and loop were closed a week later and Strichen station was no more. A path winds its way through the trees that now sprout between the two platforms and out of sight on the left the main building is still there.

The single platform station at **Mormond** on 6th July 1950 with a D41-hauled passenger train approaching from Fraserburgh. The main building here, with domestic accommodation above, was almost identical to Newseat on the line to Peterhead. Goods facilities were provided at one time but these were withdrawn in June 1940. Passenger trains continued to stop on request until they were withdrawn over the entire line in October 1965. Unsurprisingly the substantial old station building has been converted into a rather solid looking dwelling house. The platform and overbridge at the north end of the station are still there.

The neat little wayside station at **Lonmay** looking north in the 1960's. The platforms look well kept so it is very likely that the station has not yet been unstaffed. There was a small goods yard behind the signal box but that was closed in March 1964 and then lifted. As a result of diminishing traffic and the forthcoming withdrawal of passenger services Lonmay signal box closed in January 1965. Little remains at Lonmay today although the up platform is still there below the thick undergrowth.

A very early view of the station at **Rathen** with a mixed group posing for the camera. The stationmaster is in the centre in front of the platform door and the porter with a heavily laden three-wheeled platform barrow is on the left. Commonplace then but not nowadays, there are two lads with shotguns on the right. There is a signal box on the left which housed just a ground frame and, behind the platform, a standard GNSR wooden goods shed. Again the building has been converted into a house today but has been almost doubled in size. The old clock has been replaced by one of a more modern design but the lamp bracket affixed to the wall is still there, minus the lamp.

The single platform halt at **Philorth** looking north on 12th July 1950 with a short passenger train hauled by a D41 arriving from Fraserburgh. At this time there was a wooden porch to the building on the platform side. Although opened along with the rest of the line in 1865, Philorth was a private halt for Lord Saltoun and only available for passengers with His Lordship's written permission until 1926. It remained in use until the passenger trains were withdrawn in 1965. Today the station building is a house and the rather short platform is still in place. Parts of the old level crossing gate posts also remain.

In this view of **Philorth** taken from a passing northbound goods train in July 1969 the wooden porch originally provided on the platform side had been removed. It was quite a large building but this was no doubt due to the specification set by Lord Saltoun to accommodate the various waiting rooms and facilities he deemed necessary. Today the very short nature of the platform can easily be seen as can the dead straight nature of the track bed southwards.

Looking towards the buffer stops at **Fraserburgh**, or 'The Broch' as it is locally known, from left to right the extensive layout includes the two road engine shed with turntable, two main line platforms, the bay platform for St. Combs trains, the goods shed, the British Railways goods offices built in the early 1950s and the loading bank. Fraserburgh was one of the busiest freight terminals on the GNSR outside Aberdeen with fish traffic being the main commodity despatched. The lower photograph from 1983 serves to illustrate how, within two decades, Fraserburgh changed almost beyond recognition. It is doubtful that anyone working or staying there at the time could have foreseen such a scene of complete and utter devastation. The station itself had already been demolished and only the engine shed, BR goods offices and loading bank remained.

The photograph above is from nearly the same viewpoint as the previous pair of photographs but this time in colour. Steam is still in use but the yard is quieter. Rather unfortunately in today's view the overbridge has been removed so it was impossible to get exactly the same angle. However, the removal of **Fraserburgh** station from the map has to all intents and purposes been completed. Out of sight to the left the old engine shed is now used by a fish processing company and on the right, the British Railways Goods Offices is the local Council's Social Services base.

The engine shed at **Fraserburgh** in the 1950's with Standard Class 2 No.78045 on the turntable road. The St. Combs line was worked by the very similar LMS Class 2 2-6-0s, but normally they were fitted with cowcatchers to meet the requirements of the unfenced light railway. However, several locomotives without cowcatchers, including No.78045, were recorded in the 1950s on the branch when one of the regular engines was not available. Moving on to today's view the shed is still there, re-roofed and in remarkably good condition despite being almost completely destroyed by fire some years ago. It is now a fish/shellfish processing and storage unit for Iceberg Ltd, a wholesale fish merchant. The windows, right hand door and ventilator have been almost completely blocked up and the left hand door now has a roller shutter. The bothy at the back of the shed is still there but of the turntable there is no trace.

The passenger terminus at **Fraserburgh** with Standard 4MT Tank No.80005 ready to leave with a train for Aberdeen in 1954. The St. Combs branch coaches are sitting in the bay platform with its engine no doubt over at the shed for coaling and watering. Standing in almost exactly the same spot you will see that not a single trace of the station remains today. Only the tower of the Dalrymple Hall serves as a reference point to the earlier photograph.

Having covered the line all the way to Fraserburgh, we return to **Ellon** for the branch to Boddam, always knows as the Cruden section. The branch platform at Ellon circa 1930 is shown above with the London & North Eastern Railway Sentinel steam railcar *Highland Chieftain* on a working from Aberdeen. The Cruden section generated very poor financial returns throughout its existence and passenger services were withdrawn on 31st October 1932. Goods traffic lasted until 7th November 1945. The main line was to the left of the building and the fairly extensive goods yard were on the right. For a brief moment you might think there is no link with the past here but when you look at the same location today the branch platform is still pretty much intact, clearly defined by the boundary fence which curves to the left.

PITLURG 15/8/04 *Aberdeen train leaving* Porter, Photographer, Aberdeen
GREAT NORTH OF SCOTLAND RAILWAY

Operational photographs of the Boddam branch are very rare indeed so to find this postcard of an Aberdeen train arriving at **Pitlurg** at the turn of the last century was akin to finding railway gold. Pitlurg was a standard Great North wayside station with crossing loop, small yard and goods shed. The yard does not seem to be particularly busy but there are at least five coaches on the passenger train. When James Stevenson visited the location for the photograph below in the 1950s the station had been almost wiped from the face of the earth. The loading bank could still be seen though, as could the platelayers hut to the left of it and the course of the line curving away towards Hatton. Fast forward to 2017 (inset) and absolutely no trace remains. Due to the growth of trees and vegetation around the original standpoint it was almost impossible to get this shot.

Hatton, from Station

The single platform station at **Hatton** in Great North days with the village behind. There's a pony and trap entering the goods yard and another waiting for business outside the station to the right of the building. The standard GNSR goods shed behind the station platform, very similar to Blacksboat on Speyside (see page 145), lasted for many years after the line closed as it was used by the adjacent bakery. It was removed in 2009 when the site was redeveloped. Today almost the entire area is occupied by housing with no trace of the station remaining. The only recognisable feature is the Church spire in the distance and the gable end of the building on the extreme right.

This is a more a 'Then, Then and Now' and clearly illustrates the demise of the once elaborate station at **Cruden Bay** where, in the top photograph, a GNSR passenger train for Aberdeen has just arrived. This larger style of station was built to serve not only the local community but the nearby Great North of Scotland Railway owned Hotel and 18 hole links golf course. A one mile

long narrow gauge electric tramway operated by two 4 wheeled trams connected the station with the hotel. Sadly the main building at the station was destroyed by fire during repainting work in 1931 and by the time passenger services ceased only the waiting room on the former down platform remained, bereft of its canopy. The station had become a shadow of its former self. In the centre photograph taken in the 1950s only the Aberdeen-bound platform can be made out but now the Agent's house can be seen in the distance which, in the lower photo, is the only surviving landmark associated with this once proud station.

The lavish 75 bedroom **Cruden Bay Hotel** in its heyday. Note the masts for the electric tramway to the railway station curving away on the right-hand side. The hotel opened in March 1899. After the Boddam branch closed to passenger traffic in October 1932 access to the hotel became problematic so in 1934 a Rolls-Royce car was purchased by the LNER to convey guests from Aberdeen. When World War 2 broke out in 1939 the War Office requisitioned the hotel. Sadly it was never reopened and was subsequently demolished. The north east haulier Charles Alexander procured some of the stonework to use in the building of his own house near Johnshaven and due regard was paid to the design of the original hotel in the construction of his house (inset top left and bottom right). The GNSR-built pavilion also survives below the site of the hotel which is now occupied by the golf course club house. One of the electric tram bodies was rescued and given a new underframe. It can be seen at the Grampian Transport Museum in Alford. The main picture here was discovered in the GNSR coach which has been beautifully restored at Cromdale station on Speyside.

An old general view of **Boddam** from the south west showing the railway approaching the village. The station can just be seen on the top left hand side along with carriage, goods and engine sheds. The signal box is on the near side at the station throat. From the same vantage point today it is generally only the older buildings and lighthouse that can give you reference points. Look closely though, the north abutment of the old underbridge on the approach to the station in the middle of the photograph is still there.

The station building at **Boddam** photographed in the 1950s by James Stevenson. This was quite an elaborate structure and, so far as the Great North is concerned, unique in design. The tracks in the foreground had been removed after the passenger trains ceased. At one time five trains a day served Boddam but by the end this had been reduced to only two. In October 1932 services were suspended 'for the winter months' but they never resumed and were officially withdrawn in June the following year. Goods traffic lingered on until 7th November 1945. That should have been the end of it but the closed branch was used for the storage of wagons due for repair or scrapping until it was finally lifted towards the end of 1950. The station site has been completely built over now and nothing remains here to show a railway station once served the local community. The present day buildings were formerly part of RAF Buchan, an Air Defence Radar Unit, and are now used by private enterprises following reduction in the status of the Station. One station was replaced by another but it seems that anything using that term has a limited lifespan here.

Turning now to the Peterhead branch, the first place to note was **Abbey of Deer Halt**, seen above in July 1954 looking west. It was just under three miles from Maud Junction. Other than the basic slabs at the trackside provided in the late 1950s on Speyside this must surely be the smallest halt on the GNS system. It was not an advertised calling point and was used by arrangement for pilgrimages to the Roman Catholic Abbey. No opening or closing dates are recorded but it was in use in the 1930s and 1940s. In today's view there are unsurprisingly no traces of it; even the overbridge has gone. The Formartine & Buchan Way footpath occupies the old track bed.

A last day photograph of **Mintlaw** on 1st May 1965 with a North British Type 2 D6152 (later Class 21) in almost pristine condition calling with a passenger train on its way from Peterhead to Maud Junction. By this time the crossing loop had been removed although stationmaster Mr J Esslemont and his staff were still gainfully employed. This was a very difficult location to get a good 'now' shot such was the encroachment of trees and vegetation. In fact since this picture was taken the station building, which was renovated for commercial use in the 1980s but subsequently become derelict, has been completely demolished.

This cutaway cottage is immediately to the west of **Longside** station which can be seen through the road bridge. The only other example of the railway taking the corner off the side of a house on the GNSR was the Old Ferry Inn at Cambus O'May on Royal Deeside. Although the railway and the Longside Road bridge have gone, the now renovated and extended cottage is still there. Note the old wagon body in the original photo and Bridgend occupation crossing in the foreground.

Longside station looking towards Maud. Both platforms are still *in situ* with the eastbound one now occupied by several new houses. All the original buildings, bridges and associated railway paraphernalia have gone. The well-used Formartine & Buchan Way now occupies the track bed. Longside was once the junction for the short branch to Lenabo Royal Naval Airship Station. The original photo was taken on 30th August 1957, when the platform fencing and up side waiting room had already been removed.

Newseat looking east in April 1965. This was a single platform passenger station which never dealt with goods traffic. The solid granite building was very similar in style to that at Mormond on the line to Fraserburgh and combined station facilities and station master's accommodation, a practice not common on the GNSR. It was very tastefully renovated in 1989. A short portion of the old wooden faced platform survives in front of the house. The perfectly straight track bed can still be clearly seen as can the Mains of Buthlaw road bridge in the distance. Both photos were taken from the road bridge which is also still there. Tree growth over the intervening 50 odd years has transformed the general landscape here considerably.

Inverugie in May 1969 with the Great North of Scotland Railway Association's Formartine & Buchan Excursion calling on its way back to Maud Junction from Peterhead. Inverugie was a single platform station just over 2 miles from Peterhead. In today's view trees and vegetation have changed the camera viewpoint quite considerably but it is good to see that the platform is still intact and equally gratifying is the efforts made by the new owner of the station grounds to replace the original platform fencing in a very sympathetic manner.

The original station at **Peterhead** with the stationmaster wearing the almost obligatory top hat and what may well be a passenger guard on the right in full regalia. In those far away days it seemed that the longer your beard was the greater your standing in the organisation and community – proud men indeed. Note the fine set of standard railway gates made by Harper & Company of Aberdeen which could still be seen at the majority of Great North stations in the 1960s. In this particular case the gates are actually protecting the level crossing for the harbour branch, the course of which is still identifiable in many places today. Also note the hoist for unloading wagons in the background and the passenger coaches to the left of the station building. In today's view the station has vanished completely and has been replaced by Peterhead Leisure and Community Centre. The solitary point of reference between the two photographs is the gable end of the house on the left.

The station frontage at **Peterhead** in June 1954. It looks like late evening, or perhaps even a Sunday, as the main doors are firmly closed for business. Not the most attractive of stations it was functional and served the purpose for which it was designed. Rebuilding was considered before the First World War but not implemented. Latterly it had a limited passenger service of three trains from and four trains to Maud daily, except Sundays. The last train to Aberdeen left at 3.15pm in the afternoon and the last arrival came in at 5.33pm; this may not have encouraged people to travel by rail. Again points of reference today are somewhat limited; only the house on the left will help you locate where the railway station once was.

The Great North of Scotland Railway Association ran a Farewell to **Peterhead** Excursion on Saturday 5th September 1970 to mark the closure of the line to goods traffic from the following Monday. It consisted of two Mark 1 coaches hauled by Class 26 D5307. Here we see the train being propelled out from the terminus onto the single line. The engine then ran forward into the yard so that the coaches could run by gravity into the platform before setting back on top of the coaches ready for departure. Although the signal box had been closed for over 4 years the signal posts, bereft of semaphore arms, were still there and were used by several of the tour's participants to take photographs. Point rodding and signal wires were also still *in situ* so the actual position of the signal box could be readily identified. Also note the redundant Manson Tablet Auto Exchange apparatus on the right hand side at the front of the engine. In today's photo it is only the row of single storied bungalows behind the block built wall that help identify where the railway was once.

On 4th July 1951 D40 No.62272 is seen leaving **Peterhead** with a passenger train. With the abundance of goods wagons the place has a busy air to it. Many of these vans will be ready for the feast of fish traffic when it happens. The downside of course was that during a famine they would lie empty for many days waiting for sufficient landings at the harbour. The roof of the stone built goods shed can be seen above the vans behind the bracket signal. There are no points of reference in today's photograph. The new Community Centre and Peterhead Academy completely dominates the once busy railway scene.

The final Buchan branch to be described is that which ran from Fraserburgh to St. Combs. **Kirkton Bridge Halt** was located outside Fraserburgh just after the branch parted company with the main line to Aberdeen. It was popular with local golfers and the well maintained course is still there today, now incorporating some of the track bed. As with the Banff branch halts, white markers were provided at the side of the track to aid the stopping of trains after dark. It will be noted that as a Light Railway it did not require to be fenced and in the days of steam any locomotive used had to be fitted with cowcatchers. The relatively stiff 1 in 50 gradient climbing away from the halt can be easily seen in the open country ahead.

The older photograph shows a former London Transport double decker bus owned by Messrs Simpson of Rosehearty between Kirkton Bridge and Philorth Bridge halts heading for **Inverallochy,** adjacent to Cairnbulg, Competition between road and rail may have been keen but the railway provided the faster service. In today's view it can be seen that the road has been widened to incorporate some of the old track bed.

This two span bridge over the **Philorth Water** was located 8 chains (about 162 metres or 176 yards) before Philorth Bridge Halt just over 2 miles from Fraserburgh and is easily the most significant piece of engineering on the branch. The piers and abutments can still be seen today.

Cowcatcher fitted Class F4 2-4-2T No.67164, which was built for the Great Eastern Railway, arrives at **Philorth Bridge Halt** on 4th July 1951 with a service for St. Combs. The former Great North steam railmotor coaches converted for normal passenger use are included in the rake. The driveway for a dwelling house (out of sight on the left) has been provided over the old platform and track bed. Even the Nissen huts on the right have gone.

The level crossing on the eastern side of **Cairnbulg** station, with Cairnbulg village on the left and Inverallochy on the right. The line being a "Light Railway" level crossing gates were not deemed essential and the only protection was a discreet "Trains Cross Here" sign with a small red warning triangle above. Several serious accidents occurred here including a collision between a train and a double-decker bus in 1946 fortunately without fatalities. Today such crossings would have red/yellow flashing lights and yodel alarms activated by approaching trains. Even then, there have been several unfortunate incidents at such crossings and they are now being equipped with half barriers. Today, as might be expected, the housing has changed little over the years.

A two car Cravens Diesel Multiple Unit bound for St. Combs calls at **Cairnbulg** on 21st September 1963. A healthy number of passengers are disembarking no doubt having come from Fraserburgh. The branch was relatively busy right up to the end given that most stations were handy for the local population. Cairnbulg did have a rounding loop and goods yard but with the advent of the diesel units these were lifted both here and at St. Combs creating in effect a 5 mile long siding – one of the first 'basic' railways.

St. Combs looking towards the buffer stop at the end of the line with a Cravens unit sitting at the single platform waiting for business on 24th April 1965. The station site has completely gone now with only the houses in the distance providing the reference points. Even the land in the foreground has been re-profiled. The station house on the left, now partially hidden by shrubbery, is still there though. To match the 1965 shot, the photographer would have to stand in a private garden.

The original building at **Lethenty** appears to have been a simple hut. Improvements were needed but it was not until after the First World War that the platform was rebuilt and a new wooden building provided. The quality of the workmanship can clearly be seen in the recent view of the platform. Any tradesman would be proud that his work had survived still looking good after a century.

OLDMELDRUM BRANCH

This short line from Inverurie was the first branch from the Great North main line to open and, conversely, the first to close to passenger traffic. The convenience of the competing direct bus service to Aberdeen was no match for the longer journey and change of trains via Inverurie.

Goods traffic survived until 1965 and today large sections of the trackbed cannot be traced. However, the station site at Oldmeldrum is quite evident. Some of the original buildings survive although now hemmed in by new ones.

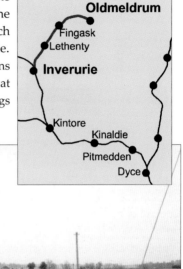

Because the Oldmeldrum Branch lost its passenger trains as long ago as November 1931 photographs of places like the unstaffed halt at **Fingask** when in operation are very rare. However, one diligent photographer took the upper photograph on 22nd October 1954 when goods trains were still running. Available historical records indicate that the platform

was beyond the level crossing on the left hand side and an apparent mound of earth in the down cess in his photo confirms that. An excellent point of reference here is the remarkably surviving concrete level crossing gate posts on both sides of the old line. One unfortunately rather grainy photo exists of the halt in operation showing that it had a name board and simple waiting shelter.

Oldmeldrum station building in its original location at the branch terminus in 1959. Passenger services were withdrawn in 1931 but the building remained in railway use. After final closure in 1966 it was in commercial use for many years. When it was no longer needed, the Royal Deeside Railway Preservation Society bought it and moved it bit by bit to their headquarters at Crathes on Deeside where a completely new station was being built. The end result is shown in the recent colour photograph below. To satisfy modern building regulations some internal alterations had to be made but the final result is very pleasing indeed.

ALFORD BRANCH

This branch ran from Kintore on the main line to the village of Alford, which actually grew up after the railway reached there. Kemnay was the only significant station on the line. Several granite quarries near Kemnay and Tillyfourie were served but otherwise traffic was mainly agricultural. Passenger usage declined quickly after competing buses were introduced and the service was withdrawn in 1950. Freight service survived until 1965 after which the track was lifted.

Parts of the trackbed have disappeared into adjacent fields and are hard to trace but, uniquely in the north of Scotland, a section near Kintore has been converted for private use by lorries from one of the quarries. These can be seen thundering along at speeds much greater than the trains would have done.

Of the stations, a couple survive as does the former carriage shed at Alford which is now used by the narrow gauge railway there as a locomotive shed.

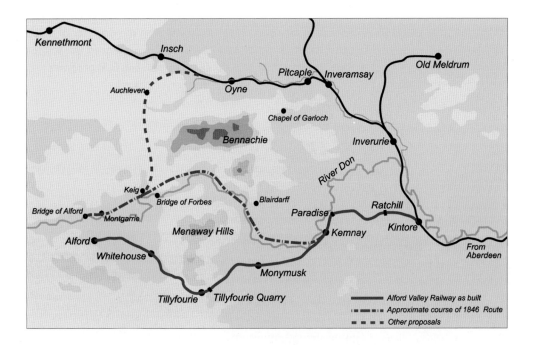

Kintore looking east on 2nd June 1959 with the main line from Keith to Aberdeen on the left and the Alford branch bay platform and release crossover on the right. All the trappings of an operational station are in place, buildings, footbridge, platforms lamps, small flower beds and seats. The footbridge is aligned to guide people coming off the branch train over the line to join their connecting service to Aberdeen. In today's view the face of the branch platform bay can still be found as a westbound service flashes past on the main line with the majority of those on board oblivious to that fact that a station, never mind a junction, existed here. But it's not all bad news as work to re-instate the station and re-double the main line is in progress.

Paradise Halt and **Kemnay Quarry** sidings looking towards Kintore. An aerial ropeway brought stone down from the quarry. It was despatched from here to all parts of the United Kingdom and although the streets of London are not paved in gold there's a fair amount of Kemnay granite to be found by those who care to look around. The short platform on the left was used by quarry workers to get to and from work. The siding here ran parallel to the single line for nearly ¾ mile with no less than three crossovers, the centre one being visible here. The first crossover was at Dalmadilly bridge in the distance and the last at the Kemnay end of the siding. As can be seen a siding was also provided with a set of double gates and ran over the road, past the weighbridge and under the tower where stone ballast for the railway was loaded. Road traffic could be held up if a set of hopper wagons was being dealt with. In today's view the now re-aligned road comes right over the old trackbed and platform. The loading tower, weighbridge, boundary wall and gates have vanished in recent years.

Kemnay during its final years of operation looking east towards Paradise Halt and Kintore. The general decay is apparent and fairly typical of many north east lines in their dying days. As an economy measure most of the wooden copes have been removed from the overgrown platforms and only those in front of the buildings retained. The small waiting room or verandah on the eastbound platform was a remarkable survivor given that passenger trains had ceased to run 15 years previously. The Alford branch was an enclave for lower quadrant signalling right up to the end. The porch on the front of the main building housed the signal box. This was unusual on the Great North of Scotland; only Woodside on the main line out of Aberdeen and Holburn Street on Deeside were similar. In today's view which was very difficult to line up the only point of reference is the house with the two chimneys on the left. The entire station area has been built over and no trace of the railway infrastructure remains.

An evocative 'ghosts of' picture at **Monymusk**. The subtle amalgamation of the 'then and now' views creates a thought provoking image. Mr McHardy, the agent, and his staff pose on the platform in the 1920s. He was a man of stentorian voice who allegedly when bellowing 'Monymusk' could make all the crows roosting in nearby trees take flight! Monymusk was always a single platform location which had a fairly busy goods yard on the right-hand side behind the cameraman. Copious amounts of felled timber from the surrounding forests were despatched from here over the years. The view is looking west towards Tillyfourie and Alford.

TILLYFOURIE. G.N.S.R.

This is **Tillyfourie** looking west towards Whitehouse and Alford, once a major granite quarrying centre. As can be seen a crossing loop and two signalboxes and full signalling were provided here at one time but these were removed in 1933, some 17 years before passenger closure and at a time when the local granite industry was in decline. The goods sidings remained though and this facility was not withdrawn until late 1952. The station building still survives as a private dwelling but the platform face has long gone. The railway cottage on the left in the older picture also still survives, although it is hidden from sight in today's view by the inevitable tree growth that has often frustrated this project. The former eastbound platform waiting room also survived for a period after been moved to the garden of the station house.

Whitehouse looking west towards Alford in 1959, taken from the guard's van of the returning branch freight. Like Monymusk this had always been a single platform location. The goods yard on the right hand side seems to be very busy, but looks can be deceptive as most are stored wagons used seasonally e.g. for potato or perhaps sugar beet traffic, or waiting attention at Inverurie Works. This storage arrangement would often be found at lightly used outstations on the Great North. The goods yard site here is used by a scrap merchant. The old station building may have been used as offices for the firm. In today's view absolutely no trace can be found of the railway.

The approaches to **Alford** station with a Class D or E 0-6-0T hauled passenger train arriving
from Kintore is the feature of this Bill Emslie watercolour which was based on an original
photograph taken before 1914. The signalbox and track layout survived almost intact right up
to the end in January 1966, the only change was that the engine shed in the distance was taken
out of use, its roof was removed and the track simplified after passenger closure in January
1950. Looking at today's view you really have to dig around to find any trace of the railway
but if you look closely the base of the signalbox has been used as part of the foundations for
the gas storage tank

An attractive group photo of the engine crew and station staff on the platform at **Alford**.
The view is looking east around the beginning of the twentieth century. The Stationmaster
is wearing a bowler hat as befits his position in the hierarchy. In today's view all that remains
is the actual platform which now forms part of the narrow gauge Alford Valley Railway.
The wooden extension in the top photo disappeared when the original stone building was
extended in the early 20th century. It was all demolished when the new structure was built
by Grampian Regional Council for the Alford Valley Railway. The AVR curves away to the left
whereas the old standard gauge line went straight ahead towards the bungalows which have
been subsequently built over the track bed.

The junction station at **Inveramsay** in 1965 looking towards Turriff with the main line to Keith on the left. A diesel shunter hauling the return working of the daily goods to Turriff has just been given authority to enter the station by clearance of the Up Branch Home Signal and will thereafter commence shunting before carrying on to Inverurie. Note the open wagons and the loading bank between the station building and the shunting engine, also the abundance of lower quadrant signals – the down main starter towards Pitcaple has a sighting board behind it. Carriages are stored in the yard on the right. Inveramsay was often used to store surplus vehicles, in some cases destined for repair at Inverurie Works. Despite having been closed to passengers since October 1951 the footbridge is still there nearly 14 years later. The quarry on the hill in the distance looks relatively new and busy. The station building is one of life's real survivors today having been reduced to a goods office then used as a bothy. It was derelict before the end was removed so it could be used as garage. The old loading bank and branch platform survive and the pole to the right of the building has been renewed and telephone wires greatly reduced.

The caravan is home to a local purveyor of quality potatoes.

MACDUFF BRANCH

The Macduff branch wandered in a generally northwards direction from Inveramsay, just north of Inverurie, via Fyvie and Turriff to Macduff where the terminus was perched on the hillside above the town.

The line was opened in stages. It reached Turriff in 1857 and then in 1860 was extended to a terminus at Gellymill to the south of Macduff. Finally, it was completed the short distance to Macduff in 1872. Although through trains were operated to Aberdeen, road competition saw its use decline in the 1920s but passenger trains survived until October 1951. Goods services were cut back to Turriff in 1961 and the whole line closed at the beginning of 1966. Today little remains. One early casualty was Plaidy, which closed in 1944. The site had been cleared by the mid-1950s and no photographs of it have been found, so it is not possible to illustrate it.

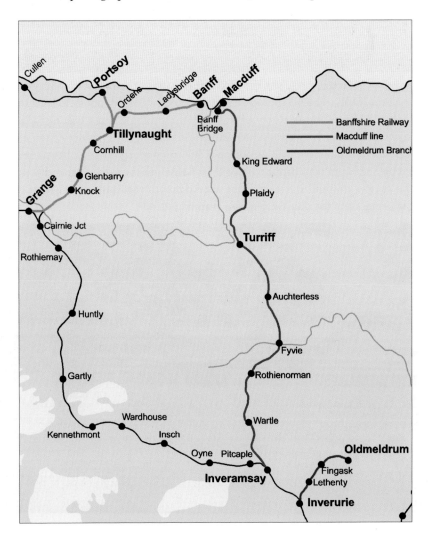

An early view of **Wartle,** originally called Warthill, with a Macduff bound passenger train arriving. The time looks to be 4.55pm and if so this could be the 4.47pm from Inveramsay due in at Macduff at 5.52pm. There's plenty of traffic on the station barrow waiting to be loaded. Advertising hoardings are lying against the wall of the building. This has now been converted into a handsome house but the former outline is still easily recognisable. It has to be said that the current owners were very happy to have their house photographed, especially when they realised the reason why and this welcoming approach was replicated throughout the work on with the project and for that we are very grateful indeed.

An attractive colour view of **Rothienorman** with a Cravens DMU working the Branch Line Society Railtour around north east branches on 5th June 1965. The unit has just arrived on its way back from Turriff, which by that time was the terminus of the branch. A good mix of upper and lower quadrant signals survived here. Note the weeds on the up platform and the base of the old waiting room on the right; passenger trains had finished here nearly 14 years before. It is difficult today to imagine a station being here at all, the only common feature seems to be what is left of the trees on the left and the power lines on the right. A car sits where the signal box used to be and houses occupy the former track bed and goods yard beyond where the level crossing was situated.

Looking north at **Fyvie** the 1965 Branch Line Society Railtour seen earlier at Rothienorman makes a photographic stop on its way to Turriff. The whole scene (below) has been completely obliterated today although the station building did survive until the 1990s.

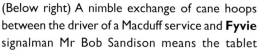

(Below right) A nimble exchange of cane hoops between the driver of a Macduff service and **Fyvie** signalman Mr Bob Sandison means the tablet for the previous section from Rothienorman has been swapped for the advance section to Auchterless. A time honoured tradition that ensured that only one train would be in a single line section between two signal boxes at any one time. A driver would lend himself liable for dismissal if he left a station without the tablet. This July 1925 photo shows Fyvie signal box on the right and, being platform mounted, it has well tended flower beds along the front. The signal box and loop were closed in 1936. Signalman Sandison was well travelled around the Great North system. Having started as lamp boy at Aberdeen in 1920 he worked at many locations including Crathes, Lumphanan, Kinaldie and Drum before retiring from his final posting at Strichen with the closure of its signal box in 1966. The scene today (middle right) is in sharp contrast to the order and strict disciplines of yesteryear.

Fyvie station looking south in 1906 when the crossing loop and signal box were extant. Judging by the quantity of parcels on the barrows and sacks lying against the fence below the metal cocoa advert a train from Macduff must be due shortly. Two members of the station staff and the station dog pose for the photographer. The station building was very similar to those provided at Wartle, Rothienorman and Auchterless; this design in brick rather than stone was only found on the line between Inveramsay and Turriff. Note that Fyvie had a staggered footbridge, i.e. up one side, across the tracks and then down the opposite way, usually found where the two platforms were not opposite each other; Kintore, Rothes and Carron were other examples on the Great North system. The roof of the goods shed can just be glimpsed to the left of the main station building. The loop, footbridge, down side waiting room and signal box were taken out of use in 1936. Today nothing remains of the station and looking from the same vantage point only the distant hills tie in with the original shot.

An early view of **Auchterless** looking north towards the level crossing. The original Great North footbridge is prominent and was unlikely to have been replaced by the LNER version before the crossing loop was taken out in 1933. The main signal box was behind the camera and was replaced by a ground frame at this time although the north box in the distance survived controlling the level crossing until the line closed completely in January 1966. The station building, albeit now extensively converted and extended into a dwelling house, is the only surviving feature but, like Wartle the basic outline can still be seen. The track bed and site of the old up platform have been completely re-profiled.

Turriff looking north in GNSR days with a service from Macduff arriving. It may well be a local Public Holiday judging by the number of intending passengers on the platform. Turriff was unique in style and a predominantly wooden structure which even incorporated a roof over the track at the north end. Note the rodding for the north end loop points running between the two lines. It was boxed in to prevent being blocked by snow; there were hard winters in these parts back then. The goods yard was on the left behind the platform fence. At first glance nothing survives today, but look closely, the stone face of the up platform is there. On the left the goods loading bank is clearly identifiable. The station area is now used as a caravan park. Turriff closed completely in January 1966.

King Edward looking north before withdrawal of passenger services in 1951. Another unique style of building, it is a simple wooden structure. The crossing loop was taken out here in January 1936 as part of the many LNER economy measures of the period. It is surprising that the basic structure of the building is still there pretty much as it was (inset) although a window has been cut into the porch at the south end. The legend 'Tickets' can still be made out above the old ticket office window. Even more surprising is that the old wagon body at the north end, which was used as a parcels store as happened at so many other GNS locations, is still there albeit in a rather dilapidated condition.

With a good head of steam and the fireman still shovelling hard D40 No.62273 *George Davidson* departs from **Banff Bridge** station *en route* for Inveramsay in early British Railways days. A stiff two mile climbing at a ruling gradient of 1 in 66 lies ahead through Gellymill and on to the summit at milepost 27. The potential for wheel slip must have been very real when a gale was blowing off the North Sea; fully operating sandboxes would have been essential. Today flowering broom covers the old railway track bed but the major features of Banff remain relatively unchanged. The former station at Banff Bridge has been a private dwelling for many years now.

Superimposing the then and now photographs, a J36 No.65338 shunts the yard at **Macduff**. The engine shed and base to the water column still survive here but all else at the south end of the station has gone. A new storage building occupies the bed of the approach lines to the shed. The non-standard signal box was perched somewhat precariously on the side of the hill and the windows must have fairly rattled when a strong north easter was blowing. The signals here were some of the first to be gas lit instead of paraffin which was normally used; maybe they didn't blow out so often.

MACDUFF FROM THE WEST.

The classic view of **Macduff** looking east from the hillside showing the complete layout as it once was with its two platforms, three sidings, loading bank, turntable, water column, engine shed and head shunt. What still survives can be easily picked out. The engine shed has been re-roofed and the former bothy at its gable end has been demolished. The church on the Hill of Doune which has been there since 1805 still overlooks the scene and will have seen a fair amount of comings and goings over the decades.

Macduff looking towards the stone built terminus on 13th June 1960. Fish vans occupy the bay platform on the left and the goods shed on the right has a sheeted wagon inside. The main building and goods shed are now occupied by Seaways Ltd and have been completely renovated to suit their purposes. The basic outline of the station still remains, including part of the window on the left and the outline ventilator below the roofline. Looking closely the inside face of the old bay platform can be seen below the boundary fence on the left.

The outside of the main building at **Macduff** in the 1950s. It was a stiff climb up to the station from the town for intending passengers. The number of chimneys suggests several offices and waiting rooms with fires to be kept burning during the winter months. Entry to the goods yard was via the metal gate on the left of the building immediately below the gable end. The building is instantly recognisable today even if the chimneys have gone and the windows on the side changed. 'The Platform' sells clothes, home items and gifts and incorporates a café.

In immaculate condition the restored No.49 *Gordon Highlander* turns on the **Macduff** turntable on 13th June 1960 while working a well-patronised Scottish Rambler railtour. Many photographs were taken on this day as the surrounding hills which enclosed the station on the south side offered great opportunities for the more athletic. A rather bland forklift truck sits where *Gordon Highlander* once stood nearly 60 years before.

BANFF BRANCH

The Banff, Portsoy and Strathisla Railway connecting Grange, on the main line near Keith, with the two coastal towns was opened in 1859. The Portsoy section became part of the through route to Buckie in 1884 and Elgin in 1886, from when Banff was just a branch from Tillynaught. It retained a frequent service of connections to Coast line trains in both directions until 1964, by which time use had fallen so much that there were no significant objections to its closure. Freight survived until the Coast line itself closed to all traffic in May 1968.

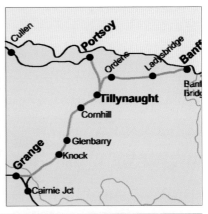

To find what actually remains at **Tillynaught,** which always was an isolated spot, requires some clever railway archaeology but searching among the undergrowth will bring dividends. Here we have a photo taken looking along the branch platform at **Tillynaught** on 4th July 1964. Having just rounded its train the Banff engine is now coming back on top of the coaches to prepare for departure along the branch again. The signal on the right with the short arm controls egress from the storage siding. Note the two inset photos. In one the stump of that signal is still there and more surprisingly in the second inset are the remains of the buffer stop at the far end of the siding. It must have been well secured into the ground because it seems to have been easier to burn off at the base of each leg rather than lift it out altogether.

In this pair of photographs the workaday scene on the branch platform at **Tillynaught** taken in 1964 contrasts very sharply with a totally unrecognizable 'now' view taken from the same location. The Class 2 2-6-0 has run round its train and is ready for the return journey to Banff. The station survived as a junction right up to the end and the main building itself lasted a few more years before being torn down and burnt to ashes by a local contractor in the early 1970s. The other end of the storage siding seen on the previous page is on the left in the view above.

Moving to the Banff end of **Tillynaught** this view on 2nd March 1963 shows the Down Branch Starting and Up Branch Home Signals. Also the Stevens flapper shunt signal which controlled exit from the branch loop on to the Banff single line which curves away into the distance. The open ground today does not really give any clue that a railway existed here at all. The only points of reference are the corner of the Station House on the left and the farm on the hill in the distance.

Ordens Halt looking east towards Ladysbridge and Banff. The colour view from 24th May 1964 shows a passenger train from Banff approaching the rather overgrown platform hauled by BR Class 4MT No.76104. The rather rudimentary waiting shelter survived for many years after closure but has since vanished; a suggestion of the old platform still remains amongst the trees and bushes. Very pleasingly the fine example of a GNSR overbridge carrying the Ordens road across the line is still there. Sharp eyed readers will note a poster on the wall of the waiting shelter; this was the closure notice for the Banff branch to passenger trains on 6th July 1964 – one wonders if the good folk of Ordens noticed?

Blairshinnoch level crossing and gatekeepers cottage on 1st October 1954. This was located just over 3 miles from Tillynaught between Ordens Halt and Ladysbridge station. After the passenger trains were withdrawn in 1964 these gates, along with all the others on the branch, were operated by the trainmen on the daily goods from Keith Junction. Today both the cottage and gates have long gone but after all these years the down side gate posts are still *in situ* (upper inset) and with a bit of close investigation, so too are the rails (lower inset) although partially tarred over. A good reference point is the road bridge over the burn in the middle distance.

Ladysbridge viewed from the south side of the line with the hospital on the hill in the background on 29th June 1906. This is yet another branch station where almost nothing exists today. Even the granite built twin sided loading bank has been removed to accommodate a driveway into a new dwelling house. The hospital has now closed and been converted into apartments but its appearance has changed little over the years other than having fewer chimneys. What is very noticeable in the sepia photograph is the number of revenue earning wagons in a very busy goods yard. In its final years Ladysbridge would only deal with occasional wagons of coal. After passenger closure, the station building was moved to nearby Whitehills where it served as the clubhouse for the local football team for a number of years.

Inverboyndie Gates were about a mile east of Ladysbridge station where the Portsoy to Banff road crossed the railway. Lower quadrant semaphore signals protected this crossing and, like Blairshinnoch, a Crossing Keeper's cottage was provided – the access and outbuildings can just be seen on the left hand side of the photograph above which dates from October 1954. Note also the Platelayers' bothy on the right hand side. Today's photograph again shows nothing has survived, even the road alignment has changed slightly which made composing the 'now' image very difficult. A walkway along the old track bed is provided today with a sensible warning to keep your dogs under control.

Bridgefoot Halt looking east with a two coach service for Tillynaught arriving in October 1963. As well as the local houses this halt, which was opened on 1st October 1913, also served the community of Whitehills although many may have preferred to continue using Ladysbridge as the fare would be cheaper from there. Being of all wooden construction it was never going to survive long after closure and nothing now remains. Note the house on the left and the roofline of the Swordanes Hotel in the distance. In 1913, automatic ticket issuing machines were brought into use here and at Golf Club House Halt which sold a single ticket for 1d for travel to either Ladysbridge, where passengers had to rebook, or Banff. Passengers could pay for First Class travel by buying two tickets.

Golf Club House Halt, near the shore about a mile before Banff, was opened on 1st October 1913 at the same time as Bridgefoot and was a request stop only. To find any trace of the track bed here is nigh on impossible but careful positioning of the photographer allows you to see where it once was. Note the white markers at the line side at either end of the platform in the opposite cess which were an aid to the Engine Driver when stopping here. The halt was generally closed for business between November and March. The inset photographs show the view looking towards Scotstoun and Banff in the far distance. The upper one, dating from 1954, shows the platform. The lower quadrant semaphore distant signal for Banff is at the end of the platform but it disappeared when the signal box at the terminus closed in May 1960. A solitary bench has been provided for passenger comfort. The gunpowder store behind the platform on the seaside is still there today and that along with a bit of fencing and the cuttings and embankments are all that remain of the scene from yesteryear.

The terminus at **Banff** in May 1964 viewed from the buffer stop. At the time the 'now' photo was taken new houses were being built on the station site. There are very few reference points other than the rock cutting on the left hand side of both pictures. The carriages are running back into the platform at almost exactly the point where the living room of the new house would be. There were no facilities at Banff to run round passenger trains for the greater part of its existence so any stock was gravity shunted into the station. Also to be seen above are the station lamps and, almost hidden on the bottom right hand side, is a dustbin clearly marked LNER.

Looking towards the buffers and the terminal building at **Banff** In July 1964. BR Standard Class 4 No.76104 is ready to leave on another run to Tillynaught where it will connect with main line services. There was no dedicated goods service on the branch; wagons were conveyed on the passenger trains to the Junction where they would later be attached to the Coast Goods. The two houses on the hill behind the station are ideal reference points and have not changed at all in the intervening years although the telephone poles have gone. Careful study of the rock formations will enable you to pinpoint where No.76104 stood.

In the early days of nationalisation D40 No.62268 waits at **Craigellachie** with a two coach train for Boat of Garten. The vintage coaches, one Great North and the other LNER Gresley design, are in the swansong of their operational life. For many years three trains each way served the communities of the Spey Valley plus one extra on a Saturday night to take the late

night revellers home. Even when the Diesel Railbus started in 1958 the general pattern remained pretty much the same. Of the three platforms at Craigellachie only part of the former very long one for the branch survives. Ample car parking is provided in the former goods yard so that walkers can head to where the trains used to go either to Dufftown or along Speyside. The rest of the station area has been landscaped and mature trees cover what was once an important junction.

From Craigellachie southward, the Speyside Way follows the trackbed of the railway. At Ballindalloch this sign for the local distillery recalls the part the railway played in the whisky industry.

Speyside Line

The Speyside Railway, often known as the Whisky line, was a fascinating route along the banks of the River Spey between Craigellachie, on the Dufftown to Elgin route, and Boat of Garten, on the original Highland main line over Dava Moor to Forres and Inverness. The Speyside Railway was opened in 1863 as the Great North's challenge to the opening of the Highland main line but was little used in its early days. The development of the whisky industry led to a growth in freight traffic such as coal, grain and draff in addition to the product itself. The area was sparsely populated and passenger services were poor. But it was well visited by railway photographers in the 1950s as the last haunt of Great North locomotives. Diesel railbuses arrived in 1958 but passenger services ceased in 1965. Goods trains lasted south of Aberlour until 1968 and the remaining section closed in 1972. Today most of the line is part of the very popular Speyside Way, used by walkers, cyclists and horse riders. At the southern end the Strathspey Railway has revived the line from Aviemore to Boat of Garten and Broomhill.

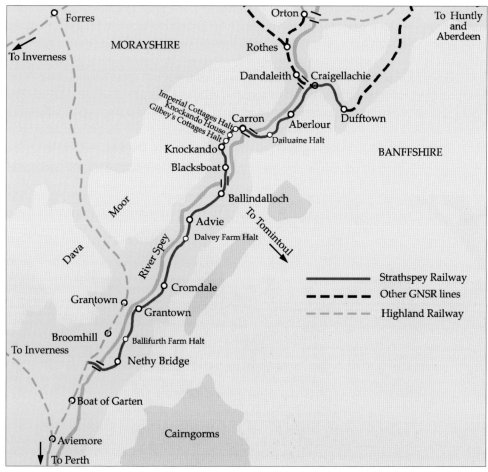

Aberlour looking south towards Carron and Aviemore. The photograph was taken in 1967, after withdrawal of the passenger trains in 1965. All the platform furniture has been removed and the poster boards are empty. Goods trains are still running but in just over a year they will have ceased south of Aberlour and in another three will have gone forever. In today's view it is pleasing to note that the now refurbished main building is still there housing a tea room and has been sympathetically extended to accommodate the Tourist Information Centre. The tracks and up platform have been removed to form part of the pleasant public park which extends down to the banks of the River Spey. The two former British Railways Scottish Region blue running in boards have been preserved; one is mounted on the end wall and the other on posts at the front of the former station building. The old Pooley weighing machine is also still there to the left of the end door.

In what looks like torrential rain Class D40 No.62275 *Sir David Stewart* leaves **Aberlour** on 10th August 1954 with a short southbound goods comprised of one mineral and five open wagons probably for whisky traffic. A brake van brings up the rear with a good fire going, no doubt to help dry the guard's clothing between shunts at the various stations. Fast forward 60 odd years and there are only two identifiable features on what is now part of the Speyside Way – the overbridge in the distance carrying the road over to Boat of Elchie and the cottage on the right with its enhanced dormer windows. The field in front of the house has now been built upon. The wider trackbed forms a car park, giving another convenient starting point to the Speyside Way.

The Distillery's own private engine shunts a wagon loaded with whisky butts at **Dailuaine**. The short branch disappearing under the overbridge in the distance came off the Speyside line just under a mile north of Carron station. The Dailuaine Pug and enginemen had authority to run on BR tracks and transferred wagons as required between Dailuaine and Carron. They also shunted at Imperial Distillery on the south side of Carron and in Carron station itself. The engine still survives and is now on static display at Aberfeldy (below) with 'Dewars' emblazoned on the side. You may or may not agree with this transformation but at least it avoided the cutters torch.

The ground frame worked connection to the exchange sidings and distillery at **Dailuaine** is shown above. The points were released by the Aberlour to Carron key token. As you can see by the milepost on the far side of this was 73 miles from Aberdeen and located between Dailuaine Halt and Carron station. Through the bridge on the right, where the 'security' gate is firmly open, were three reception sidings; these had been reduced to two by the time the line closed. The single line then continued into the Distillery itself, a total of nearly ¾ mile. The siding opened circa 1905 and closed with the rest of the line in November 1968. Today the road bridge over the siding has gone and the road has been levelled. The road bridge in the far distance is still there as are some items in the undergrowth, for example the stay for one of the former telephone poles (inset above) seen in the original photo on 29th August 1957.

Carron in GNSR days with an unusual group of men plus a dog posing for the camera. Normally such photographs would be of the stationmaster and his staff but not it seems in this case. The man sitting on the platform edge looks to be someone who has fallen on hard times and has possibly been adopted by the station staff; one can only speculate. Only the main station building and railway cottages survive today.

Carron looking towards Aberlour. A North British Type 2 (later Class 21) D6154 heads a down goods south on a chilly winter's day in October 1964. This was another busy Speyside location for freight traffic, the majority again being whisky related with its associated raw materials and coal inwards and barrelled spirit and draff out. The main building on the up, northbound platform still survives in good condition having been maintained by the local distillery during the intervening years. As can be seen the platforms also still survive, albeit filled in the further north you walk. Imperial Distillery seen to the right of the locomotive has itself been demolished but the ultra modern Dalmunach Distillery was opened on the same site in 2014.

The siding connection to Imperial Distillery was almost immediately to the south side of **Carron** station, which can be seen in the distance on the left. The sidings opened in 1897 and were served by the Dailuaine Pug which shared its duties between here and Dailuaine Distillery on the north side of Carron. The points were worked by a ground frame and were released by the Carron to Knockando key token. The connection survived right up to the closure of the line in November 1968. The brand new Dalmunach Distillery can be seen on the right through the trees in today's photo. A large man-made mound of earth which has been sown with grass seed has been created where the sidings once were. The Speyside line track bed curves away gently to the left towards the remains of Carron station. Quite a change from the early upper shot taken on 29th August 1958.

At approximately 5.15pm on 25th March 1967, two Class 24s D5070 and D5127 round the curve past **Gilbey's Distillery** north of Knockando with the Grand Tour of Scotland No.1. This tour had a mixture of steam and diesel traction throughout its travels that also included the Waverley and Strathmore routes which like Speyside were soon to close completely. Today the distillery is well kept and it is nice to see the loading bank and crane are still there and looked after. The old track bed forms part of the very popular Speyside Way.

A general view of **Knockando** looking north on 22nd June 1957. This neat station was one of the very few on the Great North that had a subway, which was at the north end, to connect the two platforms. The station was attractively situated overlooking the River Spey. As well as a three road goods yard and shed behind the signal box there was a connection to Tamdhu Distillery. Knockando was a busy place for whisky traffic. Although the goods shed has gone the station building, which has at one time or another been a visitor centre, the concrete store and the signal box are still there. The name on the running in board has been changed to Tamdhu to tie in with the distillery. The recently repainted lever frame is still in the signal box.

Blacksboat looking south in the late 1950s when it was still staffed. The sidings look busy but what you see are wagons waiting for traffic elsewhere. Note the well-kept platform and buildings which include an old coach body, used as a store. There are whisky barrels at the end of the platform which may well be loaded onto a suitable wagon of a passing goods train. When the Diesel Railbus service started in 1958 all tickets were issued by the guard and Speyside booking offices were closed. Places like Blacksboat then became unstaffed. The station building still survives today and has been rather pleasingly renovated as a private residence. So too has the goods shed (inset) which is the sole surviving GNSR wooden shed left today.

For the great majority of us, our first encounter with the railway was through the access gates and into the car park outside the station building. Here at **Blacksboat** on 29th August 1958 all the basic fixtures and fittings of a quiet country station can be seen, the access gate, with its Great North of Scotland Railway Inverurie Works builders plate fixed to the top bar, well kept access road, station building, goods shed, loading bank and telephone wires. Looking at today's view the only real difference is the lack of track and wagons, otherwise everything seems exactly the same. In both photographs it appears that the access gate had not been shut for quite a while, certainly not judging by its slightly overgrown condition in today's photograph. Sadly the builders plate has gone.

A very good Norman Turnbull colour shot of **Ballindalloch** taken in the afternoon light in June 1968. The passenger services had been withdrawn nearly three years previously and the once well kept platforms and track are now strewn with weeds. With complete closure now only months away the signs of decay are only too obvious. The goods yard in the distance looks healthy enough, with several open wagons awaiting their consignments of whisky barrels. The platforms and main building are still there today although the goods yard has vanished under a holiday housing park. The original Ballindalloch name with letters picked out in white is still above the windows and main door but the track, footbridge, lower quadrant semaphore signal and signalbox are long gone.

Advie Station, decorated for His Majesty's Visit, 14th September 1908.

In the top photograph, the single platform station at **Advie** is decked out for the visit of King Edward VII on 14th September 1908. Some considerable effort has been made to decorate the station for what will most likely have been only a fleeting visit. The station staff pose proudly in front of their efforts in their

brand new uniforms ready for the big event. It certainly must have been a memorable day for a quiet wee place like Advie.

The middle view opposite shows Advie looking north in late 1967. Only a single daily goods train from Aviemore to Craigellachie and back again was running by this time and the station

itself had been unstaffed since the introduction of the Diesel Railbus in 1958.

When you look at today's view (lower opposite) of the almost completely overgrown platform people who are not aware of the history of the station would find it very hard to believe what had taken place here nearly 110 years before. Note that the road overbridge has been rebuilt rather than removed, so much the better for users of the Speyside Way.

The building was quite elaborate considering the small population in the area but Tulchan Lodge was often visited by the Prince of Wales, later King Edward VII. The original station of 1863 was a mile north. It was moved in 1868 but it was not until 1896 that this elaborate wooden structure appeared. It is seen to advantage in the top view on this page taken in the late 1950s from the approach road, although it is apparent that by this time the building was in disrepair. It lingered on after the line closed and was eventually demolished in the 1970s. Today, the approach track is still in use to give access along the trackbed to the local cemetery.

Dalvey Farm Halt was a very small halt, blink and you missed it, one of four request stops specially opened in June 1959 to encourage local patronage after the introduction of the Diesel Railbus which had a set of folding steps to allow folk to get on and off. When the Railbus failed and was replaced by a locomotive and coach a short ladder was hurriedly brought into use; a journey on Speyside could be quite an adventure for the unwary. The halt is actually the five railway sleepers laid into the ground on the left hand side just beyond the underbridge. Although this bridge is still there the halt has long vanished. The heavy goods vehicles visible on the left certainly underline how busy the main road through Speyside is nowadays. It is such a shame that the railway did not feature more prominently in the plans for the future. There was a station at Dalvey when the line opened, approximately 10 chains (220 yards) further north, but it closed in 1868 when Advie was moved.

Cromdale looking south in June 1962 with the joint SLS/RCTS Rail tour of that year behind Great North of Scotland Railway No.49 *Gordon Highlander* and Highland Railway Big Goods No.103. The excursionists are taking full advantage of the programmed stop. Cromdale had a crossing loop and a second platform at one time but this was removed in 1921. If you search diligently amongst the long grass on the site of the former up platform you will find the base of the old waiting room still there. The goods shed on the left was an early victim of demolition.

Cromdale looking north showing the station with the goods yard behind it on 29th August 1957. A short branch to Balmenach Distillery left from the rear of the yard and curved away to the right under the main road. Note the well-kept and very productive looking allotments belonging to the local railwaymen. After the line closed the main building here lay derelict and eventually in a state of almost total collapse before it was rescued and after some considerable effort was renovated by one of our Association members. As you can see from today's view it is well worth a visit as the building, platform and the immediate surrounding area pay homage to the old Great North. Those of you with a keen eye will also note that there's even an old GNSR coach behind the platform tastefully converted into holiday accommodation.

At the end of the short branch from Cromdale station lay **Balmenach Distillery** and, like Dailuaine, it had its own locomotive which transferred traffic to and from the main line exchange sidings. The 0-4-0 saddle tank is shunting wagons at the distillery which itself has changed quite a bit over the intervening years with some relatively modern looking buildings having been demolished. The Balmenach engine now resides in storage on the Strathspey Railway at Aviemore (inset) and is unlikely to be steamed again. The Dailuaine and Balmenach pugs were among the last examples of steam in northern Scotland.

A pleasant colour shot of **Grantown-on-Spey** looking north in 1967 taken again by Norman Turnbull. The station, footbridge and signal box are typical of many stations that used to be commonplace in the north east of Scotland. After closure the building lay derelict and was on the point of demolition before Revack Estate stepped in and commenced their very welcome restoration project. At the time of writing building works are well advanced and great care has been taken to both preserve and replicated the old structure. Two Mark 1 coaches now sit on track between the platforms and will provide a café/restaurant for visitors. More details on grantowneast.com.

The main building at **Grantown-on-Spey** taken from a northbound stopping passenger train in the late 1950s. There are not many people on the platform and the signalman, with tablet pouch in hand, is diligently closing the carriage doors to ensure a prompt departure. Don't the blue enamel station signs look nice? Sadly the drinking fountain has already vanished and has been replaced by the standard tap. In today's view the work being undertaken by Revack Estate can clearly be seen. Their attention to detail includes getting the right shade of stained glass for the replacement windows.

Two BR Standard Class 4s Nos.76104 and 76108 working a southbound excursion call at **Grantown-on-Spey** in April 1961. As can be seen in today's view the works include genuine trackwork and the provision of two former passenger coaches which will be used as part of the visitor centre. A footbridge is also planned to enhance the location.

Nethybridge looking south in 1964 by which time the station was no longer staffed. The public road level crossing in the distance was formerly protected by semaphore signals which were operated by the station staff. After de-staffing these signals were removed and the crossing was opened and closed by the fireman or guard of each train. The building survives today as a bunkhouse and is in very good condition. Much of the original woodwork and stained glass has also been preserved. Speyside buildings have fared much better than most on the Great North system. Nethybridge is a particularly fine example.

Boat of Garten looking south with the SLS/RCTS Railtour of June 1962 hauled by GNS No.49 and HR No.103 calling on its way north. The signal for the Speyside line has been cleared but meantime the passengers have taken the opportunity to get some photos before they head north east. That signal and the associated crossover which can just be seen in the foreground were added for the introduction of the diesel railbuses to allow them to run through from Aviemore. Now preserved and operated by the Strathspey Railway not much has changed; the footbridge is at the opposite end of the main building, the junction semaphore bracket signal has been removed and a new water column provided. Strathspey stalwart Ivatt 2MT No.46512 *E.V.COOPER ENGINEER* is seen in the present day view.

A pre-1923 view of **Boat of Garten** looking north. Speyside trains departed from the platform behind the southbound platform building and there seems to be a train for Craigellachie ready to depart. Note the old GNSR engine shed in the distance through the footbridge. A bit of a change today as the up platform building was replaced by a simpler structure in the late 1950s and a brand new water tank occupies the spot once occupied by the carriage shed.

INDEX